MW01282275

ISBN: 9781795288781
Imprint: Independently published

52 Weeks of Inspirational Quotes

LIFE a delightful resource offering concise messages of love and inspirational quotes.

Heart to Heart

The promises that God has for our lives are not always clear. Sometimes, it's easier to understand what He has for us when we take time out of our busy schedules to establish a better relationship with Him. Trusting God's plan for our lives resting on the faith and belief that He will provide more than what we could ever imagine. The question we need to ask ourselves is, "Do we apply our heart and mind to seek God's wisdom?"

There is peace in the stillness of God.

Pathway to Joy

There is nothing more inspiring than witnessing joyful moments in someone else's life. Times like these provide a sense of awareness in our own lives of how God provides joy in the midst of all things. When we embrace the spirit of joy, we are opening our hearts to others and the ability to experience God's creation in a more meaningful way. The fact is, joy provides us the motivation we need to be happy.

"A joyful heart is the inevitable result of a heart burning with love." Mother Teresa

Unmatched

Connecting with others to an honest competition has its rewards. Typically, the first thing we do is take hold of instructions to ascertain the game is played correctly. Then we tend to strategize our opponent, while focusing on the win. In many cases the moment can be fueled with extreme competitiveness. Decorum is key as it pertain to the game, but it's only one aspect of the competition.

Integrated aspects of emotions motivates us to win. For the Bible says, "Know ye not that they which run in a race run all, but one receiveth the prize? So run, that ye may win.
(I Corinthians 9:24)

Endless Paths

All inspiring wish lists are some of the things we dream about. Of course our shining light are our families, friends, pets, and more, but learning and exploring unimaginable interest allows us to stretch our wings; it keeps us from being lockdown in an unenthusiastic cycle. Whatever our appeals in life, a piece of heaven on earth lends itself to delights we could never imagine.

Live life with a passion for new discoveries.

Blueprint

Many times, we have a tendency to rely too heavily on others' opinions instead of tapping into our own intuition. It's the responsibility of others to express their concerns, but it is our responsibility to ask ourselves, "What is God's plan for our life?" When we fail to allow God to use us for his purpose, we become immersed in falsehoods that undermine our values and self-worth.

God's magnificent work in our lives start with our devotion to Him.

Work in Progress

As we frequently embrace phrases such as, "would've, could've, should've," we risk the opportunity to respond to life special moments. As a result, we feel annoyed and subscribe to ploys in order to protect our own self-interest. Despite the underlying reasons for our actions, we have the ability to generate desired outcomes if we come to terms with our true self.

I can do all things through Christ which strengheneth me. (Philippians 4:13)

Expressions of Love

We should never mock, turn away, fight, or silence another person because of their viewpoint. It's wiser to learn one another's experiences so that we're able to appreciate each other's differences. The ability to have understanding allows us to love freely, while embracing the moment with optimism and promise.

"I've learned that people will forget what you said, people will forget what you did, but people will never forget how you made them feel."
Maya Angelou

Salvation

When we edify our spirit with God's true gifts, we will not be tempted by things that doesn't provide wholeness. May we come to appreciate our self-worth, so that our hearts remain open to love, joy, hope, faith, peace, prayer, meditation, forgiveness, appreciation, compassion, and not in images that evoke a false sense of security.

But seek ye first the kingdom of God, and his righteousness; and all these things shall be added unto you. (Matthew 6:33)

Rise and Shine

Embracing new things can be challenging, but once we align ourselves with support systems that are favorable to the promises of God, we will be less likely to focus on day-to-day stresses that prevent us from moving forward in a positive direction.

Teach me good judgment and knowledge: for I have believed thy commandments.
(Psalm 119:66)

Back to School

It's an exciting time for many parents who are born naturals at getting their children back to school, but for some parents it can be a time for leaning on your faith just to appreciate your child's new journey. As I write this message, I am reminded of times past of wanting to fix or immediately react as it pertain to issues involving my child. Thank God those were teachable moments that I have learned a lot from.

Trust God in unpredictable situations and be wise in everything you do.

Labor Day

As I began to shift gears with the urge of completing projects, I asked myself a question. Why is this holiday a trigger for you? The answer is, Labor Day allows me the ability to appreciate the great times I've had during the summer, but it also brings on anxious feelings that are typical in nature. But, regardless of the reason, I consider Labor Day a source of inspiration that enables me to reflect on all the things that are meaningful to me.

Treasure each moment in life.

Gift of Life

Celebrating Thanksgiving holiday with family and friends is a great way of preserving special moments. However, while we are enjoying mouthwatering foods and limitless topics of conversation, let's keep our eyes, hearts, and minds open to people in our community who are hungry, sick, abused, homeless, isolated and/or in need of clothing.

We give thanks to God always for you all, making mention of you in our prayers. (1 Thessalonians 1:2)

Genuine Love

Society may have difficulty understanding a compassionate love wrapped in joy and peace; just a dose of this type of love provides wholeness in times of despair. So, when we find ourselves distressed by life situations, let's be mindful of God's goodness, and the love He has for us.

God is the light of the world.

Rest Assured

The inability to acknowledge God's blessings in times of disappointment may have a negative effect on ourselves and the lives of others. It's only by the grace of God that we're able to exemplify his infinite love instead of allowing obstacles to dominate the relationship we have with our Lord and Savior Jesus Christ.

Let nothing separate us from the love of God.

Breathe

The error of our ways aren't meant to destroy us. Life lessons are testimonies for the journey we're able to overcome. Even the best of them have made mistakes and thought they've made a mess of their life, but by grace through faith in God disappointments have been replaced with heartfelt moments to be treasured forever.

Let nothing separate us from the love of God.

Merry Christmas

As we celebrate the warmth of this holiday season with family and friends, let's remember to pay homage to our Lord and Savior Jesus Christ by way of song, praise, gratitude, and charity. As long as the spirit of Christmas (Christ) reside in our hearts; joy, peace, hope, and goodwill will reign forevermore.

Behold, a virgin shall be with child, and shall bring forth a son, and they shall call his name Emmanuel, which being interpreted is, God with us. (Matthew 1:23)

Love Letter

Father God, thank you for the opportunity to celebrate the holiday with family and friends. We thank you for the many blessings you bestow upon us, and we praise you for your constant love. We ask that you grant us grace and mercy in times of weakness as we continue to live a life according to your word.

God is love.

Happy New Year!

Wishing you a wonderful, prosperous, healthy, New Year. May the blessing of the Lord be upon you, and may you embrace each day with the hope and belief for a better tomorrow. Cheers to a life filled with joy, peace and love!

This is the day which the Lord hath made; we will rejoice and be glad in it. (Psalm 118:24)

Open Hearts

Proclaiming God's word comes in many forms (prayer, meditation, dialogue, songs, Bible scriptures, etc.); it crosses boundaries we've never thought imaginable. Even if we have defined differences, we recognize that wholehearted believers who are called by God to share His word have similar hearts and minds alike.

Then he opened their minds to understand the scriptures. (Luke 24-25)

Honor Matters

To live a life of love is one of God's greatest gifts to man. Therefore, we must raise our voices with a song of praise to God as an expression of love for His infinite grace and mercies, but most of all for dying for our sins and giving us a new life in Him.

Let the word of Christ dwell in you richly in all wisdom, teaching and admonishing one another in psalms and hymns and spiritual songs, singing with grace in your hearts to the Lord.
(Colossians 3:16)

Fret Not

Difficulties of life may influence the way we act, feel and think, but God provides compassion and grace to assist with these worries. So, when we find ourselves becoming swayed on how we handle various situations, we must realize that God's love is greater than the confines of this world.

". . . for God sees not as man sees, for man looks at the outward appearance, but the Lord looks at the heart." (1 Samuel 16:7)

Real Talk

The preoccupation with activities that preclude the ability to contribute to the welfare of others, diminishes one's testimony. When we lose the desire to educate, inspire or empower, we send a message to the world that self-indulgence is more important than the gifts God has given each one of us.

Like clouds and wind without rain is a man who boasts of a gift he does not give.
(Proverbs 25:14)

Choose to Win

In this lifetime you will have to travel your journey alone. People will offer advice on how to prepare for your journey, but the ultimate voyage will be yours. At times your travels will place you in unknown territories which will be challenging, but don't be dismayed God will sustain and advance you throughout your journey.

To one he gave five talents, to another, two, and to another, one, each according to his own ability; and he went on his journey.
(Matthew 25:15)

Valentine's Day

Expressions of love and kindness are great ways of nurturing relationships. Although there are many ways to show a person that you care, saying 'I Love You' and 'Thank You' provides an indelible imprint to the heart. Mainstream may suggest otherwise, but the love of God's blessings pours out unto our hearts everything that we could ever need.

Precious love never disappoints.

Spellbound

Increasingly, various forms of media (radio, social media, and television) have influenced our thoughts for the decisions we face in life. Let's be aware of the reputation of the source before we embrace its philosophy which may affect our lives and the lives of our loved ones.

But when he, the Spirit of truth, comes, he will guide you into all the truth. He will not speak on his own; he will speak only what he hears, and he will tell you what is yet to come. (John 16:13)

Stay Healthy

Our health may be an aspect of ourselves that we tend to overlook. It's important that we manage our health with physical/mental exercise, proper nutrition and quiet time, so that we're able to live a life of what we love with the joy and strength for a healthier tomorrow.

Beloved, I wish above all things that thou mayest prosper and be in health, even as thy soul prospereth. (3 John 2)

Humanity

Having the right attitude is indelibly one of the most precious gifts from God. It allows one to be used by God to serve humankind. So, despite, at times, when life situations causes us to respond unfavorably, we should strive to maintain a proper attitude as we are representative of our Lord.

Let brotherly love continue. (Hebrews 13:1)

Hope

Too often, we find ourselves connected to ideals without fully understanding the subtleties and the core reason for the relationship. As stewards of Christ, we should base our decisions on quality principles so that we're not compromising our values with the need to fit in.

My soul, wait thou only upon God; for my expectation [is] from him. (Psalms 62:5)

Spring

There's no greater feeling than to have the warmth of the sun resting upon your skin; especially in the springtime. God loves to pour into our soul nature's beauty. As we attune to new day-to-day activities, may we take a moment to thank God for life's creation and the blessings we receive from them.

And he shall be as the light of the morning, when the sun riseth, even a morning without clouds; as the tender grass springing out of the earth by clear shining after rain. (2 Samuel 23:4)

God is Able

Who we are in Christ allows us to influence others through our faith and belief in God. We have the ability through prayer to strengthen families by asking the Lord to provide jobs, quality schools, work/life skills, housing, decent wages, healthcare, and safe communities. God has graced us to be a blessing to others. The question is, are we?

Thou shalt also decree a thing, and it shall be established unto thee: and the light shall shine upon thy ways. (Job 22:28)

Good News

We should never question ourselves about the love we have for Jesus or vice versa. It was God's divine plan for all his children to be accepted into his family. While some may believe otherwise, we have the assurance through God's Holy Word (Bible) that Jesus paid the penalty for our sins.

And he is the propitiation for our sins: and not for ours only, but also for the sins of the whole world. (1 John 2:2)

He Knows

A person's choice to say Easter Sunday or Resurrection Sunday is totally up to that individual. It's more important to acknowledge the death and resurrection of our Lord and Savior Jesus Christ. The true message is, Jesus is with the Father and he also remains with us all. What greater way to celebrate new life in Jesus?

Jesus said, Blessed are those who have not seen and yet have come to believe. (John 20:29)

Mourning

A heart filled with grief is a strong emotion that consumes the soul for either a short or long period of time. During this difficult time, may we find comfort in the gathering of family and friends to help us cope with the sorrow we endure and to pay our respect for our lost loved one.

Blessed are they that mourn: for they shall be comforted. (Matthew 5:4)

Good Stewards

At certain moments in life we may be asked to provide our opinion on matters related to God. During such time, we should consider sharing a few of our own experiences so that others may understand our position. With this in mind, we will remain confident in delivering God's message with others.

If any man speak, let him speak as the oracles of God; if any man minister, let him do it as of the ability which God giveth: that God in all things may be glorified through Jesus Christ, to whom be praise and dominion for ever and ever. Amen. (1 Peter 4:11)

Benevolence

Our unique qualities helps us to connect with people in different ways; it's the core reason why we are made in God's image. Our relationship with the Father and his unconditional love for us has graced us to be kindhearted, compassionate, understanding and peacemakers throughout the world.

And we have known and believed the love that God hath for us. God is love; and he that dwelleth in love dwelleth in God, and God in him. (1 John 4:16)

Something New

A person's desire to inspire another should be based upon the manner in which the message will be received; taking into careful consideration a person's emotional, spiritual and/or physically being will allow the person who is listening to identify, but not necessarily agree.

Many therefore of his disciples, when they had heard this, said, This is an hard saying; who can hear it? (John 6:60)

Victory

Each time we press through life's situations, tragedies and/or worries, God grants us savings grace so that we may praise and honor him unceasingly. This is why it's important to seek him in everything that we do. He is an amazing God who has the power to transform our lives and to make a way out of no way. We must never forget the love he has for us, because there is nothing greater than his love.

For the Lord is good; his mercy is everlasting; and his truth endureth to all generations. (Psalm 100:5)

Memorial Day

In remembrance of those who gave the ultimate sacrifice for our freedom and for the families who miss them, you are in our hearts today and every day. We also honor those who are serving in our armed forces and military veterans.

Greater love hath no man than this, that a man lay down his life for his friends. (John 15:13)

More Than Enough

Regardless of how small we think the gifts God has blessed us with, we have the capability to connect, inspire, and to improve on the lives of others as well as ourselves. The downside is, we fail to accept our gift because we consider it to be different than another person's. We should keep in mind that God doesn't make mistakes. He believes in our own ability when we may not; therefore we should focus on the things we can do and allow God to do the rest.

He telleth the number of stars; he calleth them all by their names. (Psalms 147:4)

Along The Way

It takes faith to believe in the things we do not see, but God is our guide in helping us understand the things we are incapable of comprehending. We learn to never give up when life throws us a curve ball, but instead to lean on Him with hope and strength because we realize he is in control.

Now faith is the substance of things hoped for, the evidence of things not seen. (Hebrews 11:1)

Life Lessons

There's no guarantee for the plans we make in life, but there's comfort in knowing, God is present in every situation. He loves us and cares about our plans more than we could ever imagine. Therefore, we should take heart in knowing God makes available to us the things we find difficult to conceive.

We walk by faith, not by sight.
(2 Corinthians 5:7)

Link

Our admiration for things in life have a way of connecting to times past. A sweet smell from a honeysuckle tree, a person's smile, a favorite dish, a road trip, or a song can add joy to a person's heart. Therefore, we shouldn't overly concern ourselves with life's turmoil, but embrace the things which have shaped our lives over times.

Finally, brethren, whatsoever things are true, whatsoever things are honest, whatsoever things are just, whatsoever things are pure, whatsoever things are lovely, whatsoever things are of good report; if there be any virtue, and if there be any praise, think on these things. (Philippians 4:8)

July 4th

In honor of the spirit of Independence Day many will be enjoying themselves at festivals, parades, cookouts and firework attractions. At the same time, people from other countries who had a dream of becoming a United States citizen will be taking the Oath of Citizenship. Let this day, as well as every day, be a reminder of the challenges we have overcome, the sacrifice others have made for us to have a better future than what they may have had, and last but not least that all God's children are created equal.

Hope does not disappoint. (Romans 5:5)

Unbroken

Sometimes we are overcritical of past actions which may hinder us in truly experiencing God's future blessings. May we come to know in our hearts that God's love is not based on perfection; it's impossible to live in this world without wrongdoing. We should make every effort to focus on the Word of God, so that we do not judge ourselves too harshly for the errors of our ways.

And the Lord said, Simon, Simon, behold, Satan hath desired to have you, that he may sift you as wheat: But I have prayed for thee, that thy faith fail not: and when thou art converted, strengthen thy brethren. (Luke 22:31-32)

Refuge

God is the assurance we need when our hearts are filled with sadness. As we grow in His word, we better understand his intentions for our own life. The fullness of His truths penetrates our hearts with appreciation and joy. Our pains and even our fears begin to subside because we fill our hearts with His love.

O taste and see that the Lord is good; blessed is the man that trusteth in him. (Psalm 34:8)

Servant Heart

It never ceases to amaze me how people in this world derive complete satisfaction from helping others. These people, through God's grace, help us to discover the possibilities of life so that one day we will be able to respond to others with the same kindness that was shown to us.

Blessed are the meek: for they shall inherit the earth. (Matthew 5:5)

Vision Board

At times we become disappointed because the goals we set do not happen by the time we expect them to. We should remember that God is concerned about our success and he provides the reassurance we need to remain faithful during times of uncertainty. His love is the direction we need when circumstances of life interfere with our desires.

Delight thyself also in the Lord; and he shall give thee the desire of thine heart. (Psalm 37:4)

Masterpiece

There is no need to be ashamed nor afraid to live our truths. God created each one of us in his image and for his purpose. Therefore, we should find comfort in knowing that we are more than conquerors through Christ Jesus who loves us. Even in times of uncertainty, He reveals his love in an amazing way.

O give thanks unto the Lord, for he is good: for his mercy endureth forever. (Psalm 136:1)

A Joyful Heart

The carefree days of childhood help us to understand the things that shapes our lives today. It helps us to inspire others through personal experiences that accentuate our love for simple pleasures, our hope for a better tomorrow and the importance of living a life full of joy.

Whether therefore ye eat, or drink, or whatsoever ye do, do all to the glory of God. (*Corinthians 10:31*)

Grace and Mercy

Sometimes, in the mist of uncertainty, we have to cry out to the Lord until our hearts are satisfied. With tears in our eyes, we know He is in control; with praise in our hearts, we know our prayers have been answered because we were not ashamed to call on his name.

And whatsoever ye shall ask in my name, that will I do that the Father may be glorified in the Son. (*John 14:13*)

I Do

Stomach in a knot, mind in a fog, eyes filled with tears. There's no turning back to once was. God has touched my heart through the Holy Spirit. Feeling weird but at the same time free. Even though life's direction is unclear -- I will fix my eyes on Jesus.

Be still, and know that I am God: I will be exalted among the heathen, I will be exalted in the earth (*Psalm 46:10*)

Something More

God is affirmation for the battles we are unable to conquer. Therefore, we must remain confident and commit ourselves to Him. The promises he has instore for our life will outweigh the trials we have to overcome.

Unto thee, O Lord, do I lift up my soul.
(*Psalm 25:1*)

Made in the USA
Middletown, DE
10 December 2019

80380986R00031